I Garden

Ethan Goffman

Cyberwit.net
HIG 45 Kaushambi Kunj, Kalindipuram
Allahabad - 211011 (U.P.) India
http://www.cyberwit.net
Tel: +(91) 9415091004
E-mail: info@cyberwit.net

Printed at Repro India Limited.

To Marianne

Acknowledgements

The author gratefully acknowledges the following journals for publishing versions of these poems:

Alien Buddha — "Mother Kali, Destroyer of the Multiverse, Comforts Me Who Is Callie Who Is Shiva Who Is Comforting Me"

Arial Chart – "Study in Pink" and "Why"

Blazevox – "Now Is the Far Future," "Plastic Bag," and "The Earth Is the Center of the Universe"

Bradlaugh's Finger – "The Blue Jay and the Tuxedo Cat," "Thinking of Spring in the Fall," and "Time"

Burgeon – "Mowing the Lawn"

EarthTalk – "Lines Written at Seneca Creek State Park"

Literary Yard – "Help, I Am a Human Trapped in the Body of a Human," "Poem in Limbo," "Social Justice Worrier," "Why I will never get a DNA test"

Mad Swirl – "Ellington Lives, in Heaven, in Hell, on YouTube," "Fruitflies Are Eternal, Poems Die Every Day"

Museum of Poetry – "Callie and the Rubik's Cube"

Pangolin Review – "Looking Over Wetlands"

Piker Press – "A Very Short Collection of Very Short Poems," "After We Die"

Ramingo's Porch – "Feeling the Misery of Biting Fleas," "I am nobody and I like it that way," "My Wife Eats Grapes While I Sit in the Dark," "Native Americans Return to the Suburbs," "Oh No, Not another

Nature Poem!," "Poems from the Ancients," "The Lake Isle of I'm Asleep"

Setu – "Aesthetic Delights of the Coronavirus," "Do Not Read this Poem, Read the One Below," "Don't Even Glance at This Poem, Read Only the One Above," "Thelma and the Bluejay"

Tails from the Trail (video series) – "To a Valley, *a mutant sonnet*"

Under the Bleachers – "An Infinitely Meaningless Poem," "Why I Have Wasted My Life"

Verse Virtual – "Armstrong on the Moon," "When Woody Met Annie"

Winedrunk Sidewalk – "America, America," "As Notre Dame Burns"

SPECIAL THANKS to Marianne Szlyk and Dan Morris for their thoughtful comments on the manuscript

Contents

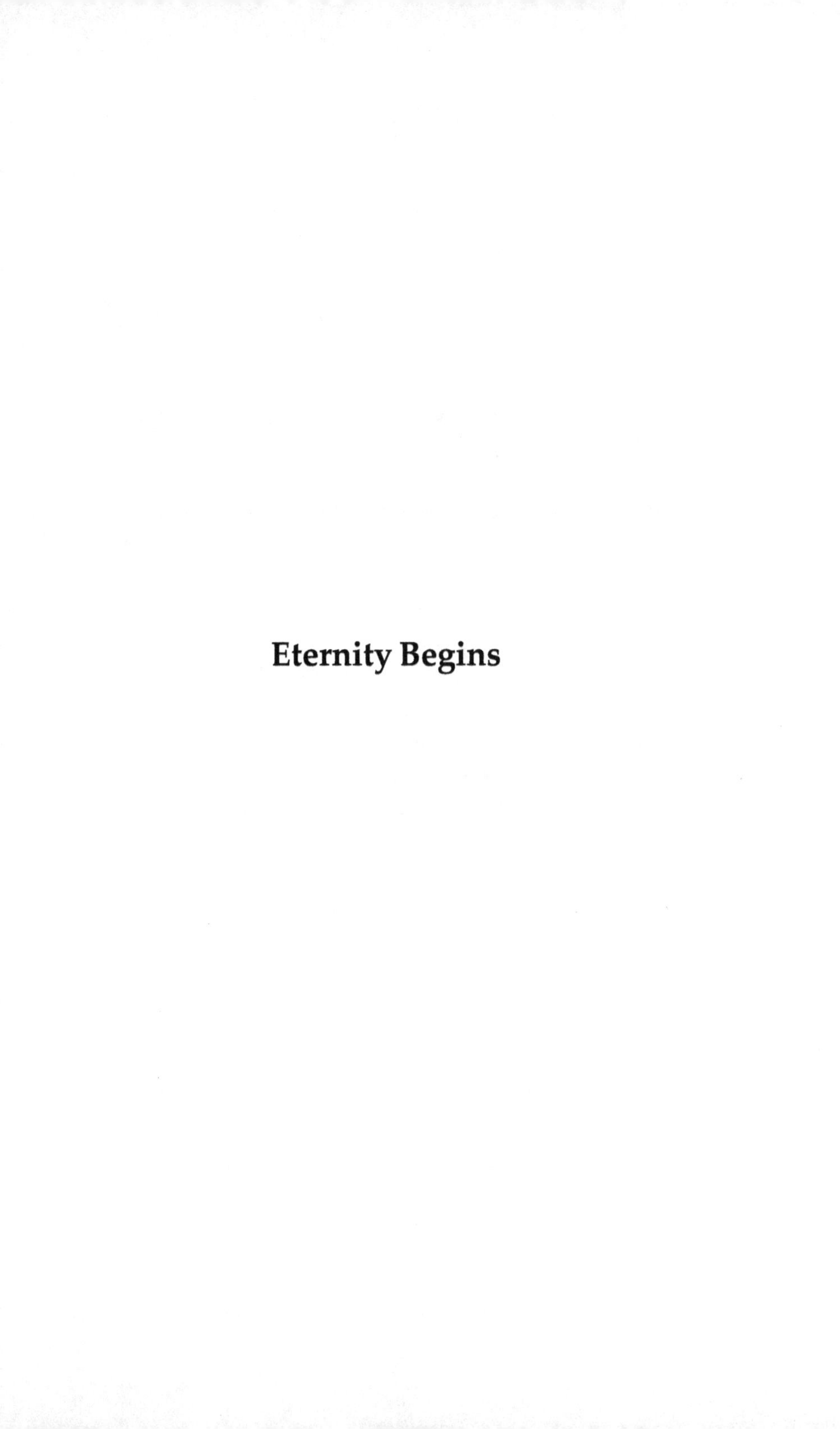

Eternity Begins

Everything Is Everything

If they have an Everything Bagel, can a Theory of Everything be far behind?

But wait, isn't a Theory of Everything necessary before one can create an Everything Bagel?

What's in the hole of a bagel? Nothing! What's the opposite of nothing? Everything! So doesn't the surrounding bagel have to be everything?

Perhaps something is the opposite of nothing. But then everything is not the opposite of something which means that everything does not exist. On the other hand, nothing is something that doesn't exist so if everything does not exist that makes it the equivalent of nothing. So something and everything would be opposites, although something is the subset of everything.

Armstrong on the Moon

They say it was Neil,
but I know better.

It was Louis
playing his golden trumpet
to the cosmos.

Louis' face gazes down
from the moon.
He sings a paean,
skies of blue, clouds curly white—
searing joy
that echoes on a million stereos,
a million streaming downloads—
to this wonderful world.

Ellington Lives, in Heaven, in Hell, on YouTube

Angels dance on piano keys,
spontaneous, blinding,
hither and yon, traversing black and white.
Perfection in motion.

The marriage of heaven and hell
gorgeous chaos, tumultuous harmony.

A horde of horns
leaps in,
a mad chase,
call and response.

Angels dance,
a garden
of forking paths,
a circuitous maze
each twist, turn, zig, zag, shuffle, leap, pirouette
perfectly planned.

This heavenly choir
satanic convergence
cackling cantankerous conversation
howls from hell to the heavens
in devious delight.

Our hosts from high and low
romance the raw repressed,
bounce and bubble,
a cacophonous choir,

Rocking in Rhythm,
summoning us all
to heaven
and beyond.

Callie and the Rubik's Cube

Back arched, hair as erect
as the leaning tower of Pisa,
Callie glares at the Rubik's Cube.
In the vast recesses of her mind,
which extends beyond human awareness of space and time,
she has solved it easily,
visualized every move,
conjured a similar puzzle in 4, 5, even 7 dimensions.

But she has
no way to manipulate
the physical cube.

Callie has poetry in her
more intricate, more passionate
than Shakespeare,
stories to tell, worlds to unfold
but no means to express it.
All she can do is
meow.

With fierce swiftness,
Callie
pounces.

The Rubik's Cube
is indifferent.

An Infinitely Meaningless Poem

As the old song goes, "nothing is real"
but how can nothing be real when it's the absence of something?

Set theory says
there is an infinity of infinities
but I say
there are no infinities
no infinity plus one;
since infinity cannot exist in the first place
and cannot even be conceived
it is impossible to add one to it.

There are zero infinities
not just because infinity doesn't exist
but because zero does not exist.
In reality
there are zero zeros.

In this way
zero and infinity are the same
sweet nothings in the human soul
and the minds of mathematicians.

How many mathematicians you ask?
A countable number
a number that exists
something, not nothing.

Nothing is not real
not unreal
not surreal
simply not
but not even not, since "not" is just another way
of expressing zero.

Still, for us humans
nothing is something
so much more consequential
than infinity.

I have no money
zero
nothing.

When you are broke
nothing is everything.

Mother Kali, Destroyer of the Multiverse, Comforts Me Who Is Callie Who Is Shiva Who Is Comforting Me

I strike a gong
summoning Kali
queen of the underworld

She hops in my lap

She's been living with me a long time
Kali
Since the day I was conceived
(which was always and never)

Kali was the egg
and Jehovah the sperm

Callie a purring ball of love

Kali is death
and Jehovah life

Jehovah is a myth
and Kali the eternal truth

Death is life is life is death
Kali is Jehovah is Kali

Mistress of life mistress of suffering
naked shimmering black and blue
too gorgeous too horrific to glance at

We pass on our sperm
pass on our eggs
to be immortal
donate an infinitesimal part of our bodies
to the multiverse

Our spawn will die
our species too
but we will live forever
and never

This seething breathing loving suffering corpse
we call self
will rot

We are empty husks of corn
scattered to the winds
since before our conception
our lives laid out
our deaths long past

We die first and are born

Kali knows intimately
that death and life
destruction and creation
are an illusion
a bitter reality

Knows time forward and backward
sideways and upside-down,
she exists yet doesn't exist outside time inside space
twisted pretzel
maze with no beginning

invoking Jehovah
I summon Kali
already here
always never existing

She is no Indian goddess
she is he is they is I
transgender and cisgender gay and straight and binary bent and
crooked liar and truth
they is mother goddess of life

His wife Shiva
his husband Kali
its spouse Kaliva
their horde of significant others Shali

Saliva
a drop of the universe

Destroyer of worlds
guardian of the multiverse
comes to me
at the echo of a gong

Saliva echoes with universes
the instant Kali spits it
spits herself
from his mouth
scattering them to the five winds

The instant of creation
the eternity of Ragnarok
preordained by the demon Jehovah
created within my destructive self
created by the universe despite my pitiful pleas
a mewling dying kitten freshly born
Shrödinger's Rubik's five-dimensional cube
Callie simultaneously alive and dead everywhere and nowhere

I strike a gong larger than the universe
the size of a hangnail
dangling from my left pinkie toe

Callie is there
a familiar from eons past
from an unimaginable future
a gift from my mother
Shiva comes from the next life
to torment me with kindness

We cannot escape
Cali
Kallie
rubbing against I
purring and soothing
tiny circle of life in my lap

She springs up
startled by a distant gong
disappears into the multiverse
leaving bloody skidmarks
in our soft flesh

I strike a gong
a gong strikes me

Eternity

The universe is a big, sad place
more than 99.9% empty
yet filled with pain and yearning.

The Earth Is God's Backyard

The Earth Is the Center of the Universe

Some say the Earth is the
     womb of the universe
The seething center, mother
     of myriad forms
Oozing with vitality, soft with soil, pregnant with being
The sticky womb of everything
     birthing its own self

The Earth, the Earth, the Earth
Not the sun
     not the Milky Way
Not some mega-cluster of galaxies too vast
     to be conceived
     by us infinitesimal earthlings
     the true titans
     that created the universe

But the Earth, the Earth, the Earth, the Earth
     the swirling center
     around which the sun, the moon, the stars, the galaxies
Revolve

Nothing exists, not primordial mists, not emptiness
     till we earthlings perceive it

Yet we, ourselves, our contemplating selves
     do not exist, did not exist
Till certain chemical process
     spun out of god knows what hell

or heaven
created us from nothing
allowing us to create
the Earth, the Earth, the Earth, the Earth, the Earth

Emptiness is not empty
Just as fullness is not full
The glass is always already
        half full, half empty, all of both

Optimism is pessimism
air rises above water
water drips down from air
earth sinks into water
water ascends from air

Air is emptiness
the nothingness without which there is nothing
an empty universe
a blank page waiting
to draw itself upon

To birth
itself

Where else would self arise?
     since nothing comes from nothing
Nothing must be something must be nothing must be something
Air must be water must be fire must be earth
     the whole god-damned table of the elements
     the whole blessed periodic table that gives us

                      life

is water is life is water

earth comes from water comes from air comes from fire comes
from potassium comes from chloride comes from uranium comes
from uranus comes from something comes from nothing comes
from something comes from everything comes from nothing

By the Wetlands My Wife Often Visits

I gaze
over the bountiful little swamp
blooming with yellow and purple flowers,
erect reeds, billowy shapes

A butterfly bounces
above the vegetation,
an angel's yellow wings

Within a flower, an intricate, sculptured bee
gathers and replenishes

On a green stalk
a spot of white,
half-microscopic organism half flits, half crawls

within the murky water
a slow turtle?
or just a rock?

On solitary journeys, my wife and I
compose poems to this wetlands,
each poem individual
of the same swampy pond
trickling words and water, ineffable
every droplet linked to every other.

I think that I shall never see
a poem as lovely as a bee.

Looking Over Wetlands, Summer, Maryvale Park

Bright flowers, yellows and purples,
ascend: angels praying.

Beneath thick vegetation,
turtles swim gracefully,
scurry with clumsy little limbs
amid the litter and pure, mucky
swamp water,

holding up Earth
on their strong backs.

Study in Pink

cherry tree weeps flowers
onto the garden.
shoots peek up
green threads
in a snowy blanket.

Mum's the Word

I planted four small mums along our fence
to delight passersby.
They might bloom soon, ablaze in crimson,
or just as easily die
as fall intersperses with winter.

So it is for life on this strange planet,
always frail, always resilient,
ready to take off, take over, overcome,
always teetering on extinction's brink.

I planted four small beings with four small prayers,
dug holes not deep or shallow, holes like graves,
like churches,
added black compost,
gently patted soil around
each small plant,
each clinging life a little shard of hope.

I Destroy Biodiversity Because the Neighbors Expect It

I mow the lawn in squares, in lines, in curving patterns, slicing violent paths, decapitating waving grassy shoots, lovely purple and yellow flowers spattered like stars, bushy violet flowers with green bonnets, snaking yellow weeds, a biodiverse array, a multicultural polyphony, sweet nectar for birds, butterflies, and bees. Why am I destroying their habitat, their sustenance? Why did the western settlers shoot down vast throngs of buffalo?

As I mow, large friendly bumblebees float by. Do they want to kiss me or sting me?

Mowing the Lawn

I come upon a corpse,
a baby bird, almost a fetus still
that likely never felt the thrill
of flight
even for an instant.

With a swift sideways kick,
I send the sad little thing
into the garden.

It will become fertilizer
nourishing
new plants
housing and feeding
future bugs
themselves food for
future birds.

Nature is cruel
nature is kind
nature runs in cycles
knowing neither kindness nor cruelty.

I cut neat
shrinking squares of wild grass
into tamed pastures
conquering the wilderness once again.

One day I will be
food for maggots
and worms.

As I end my morning tasks, I glimpse
hopping across the fresh cut grass
a baby bird
vibrant with life
ready to fly.

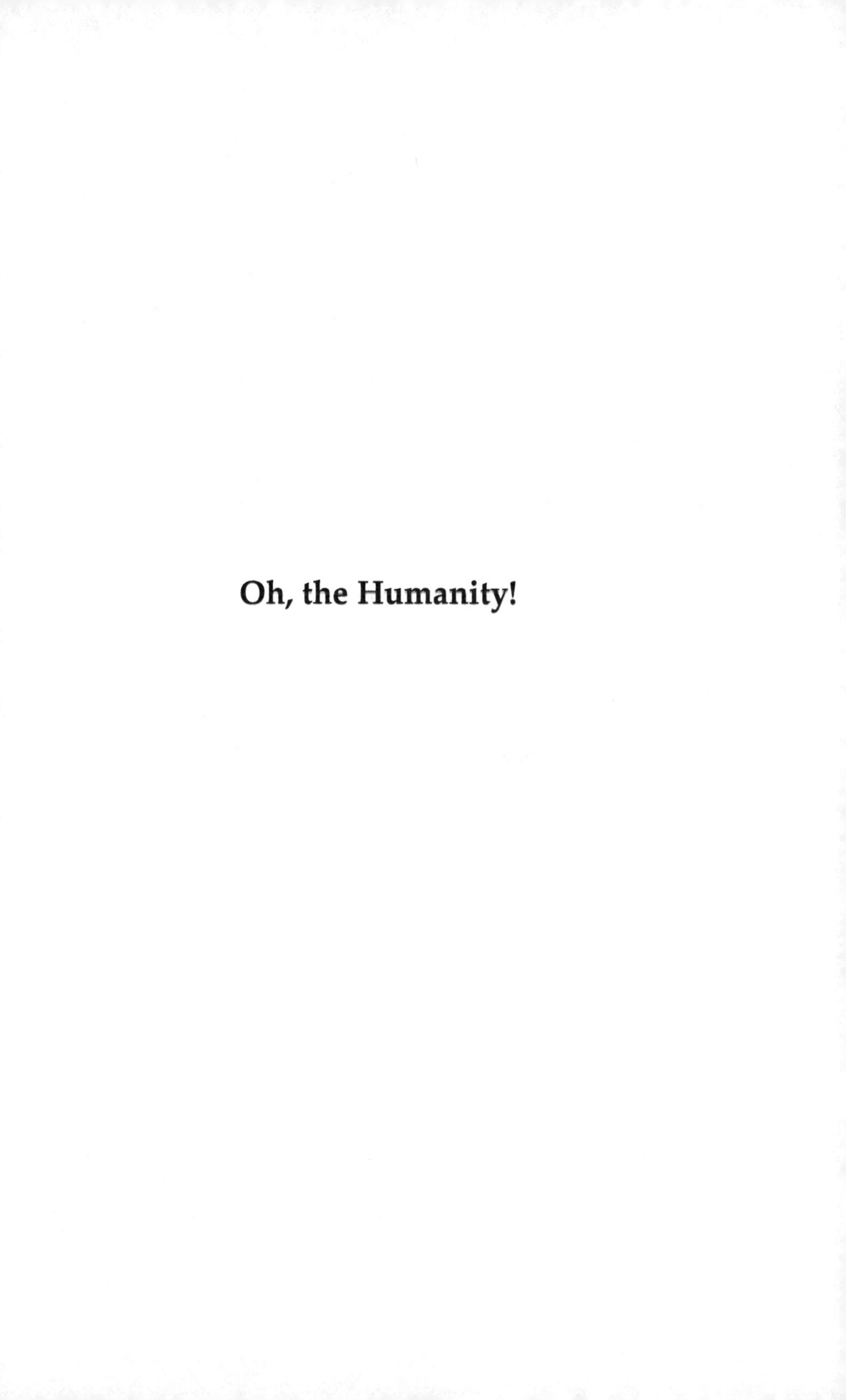

Oh, the Humanity!

America, America

I will protect you to the death
of a million Mexicans
bones bleaching in the desert.

Of 5 million Syrians
begging to be allowed to
live.

Of hundreds of Jews
packed in the hull of a stinking little boat
fleeing Germany.

America, America
the wretched refuse
washing up like garbage
on our shiny, inviolate shores.

I will build a wall to protect you,
another brick in our long history.

I guess you could call that love.

As Notre Dame Burns . . .

I am cleaning house
hoisting a mighty brass lamp
to sweep away
the accumulated dust
of eons . . .

A stupefying crash
the end of something.

The lamp's base has rotted, fallen out
lies in
scattered fragments
humpty dumpty.

This massive lamp was
a lighthouse
guiding us to safety

a thousand years of Western civilization
crashing down
burning up
the center cannot hold

vast chunks of glacier
calving off

England, Hungary, Turkey
spinning apart
the new Europe
the new world order

the ancient civilization
the global Empire
liberal democracy
neoliberalism
rot
fire.

. . .

Toss away
this bronze lamp
among the ephemera
of a new world order
built on commerce
a foundation of sand.

We order anew
Amazon Prime
dealer
for a billion junkies
flotsam from China's million factories

a foundation of
cheap labor.
. . .

The smoky remains of the ancient cathedral
wavering yet proud
an ancient skeleton.

Somehow, a miracle
The crown of thorns
has survived the blaze

now each of us must wear it.

When Woody Met Annie

Back then Manhattan glittered
an island, a metropolis, a universe
Rhapsody in Blue soaring from every window
of every skyscraper, every brownstone
breathing romance.

A couple in silhouette,
Annie towered above you.

In those days
tough guys glared
from a billion big screens,
Clint Eastwood, Jack Nicholson,
guys who took a gut punch
and stayed silent.

You were nothing like that,
a mensch, gushing
wry one-liners
epic romance
the terrible and the miserable,
the beautiful, too.

Charlie Chaplin reborn
as a giant pair of glasses,
thick black rims
quintessential nerd.

A real man is
articulate, emotional.
Annie, nervous and talkie, in her jacket and tie
so feminine
announcing
our androgynous future.

Schlimazels, intellectuals
a mismatched duo
quintessential Manhattan
quintessential America
so of your time, so ahead of your time.

You wrecked it all,
stomped on your own glasses,
stalking young girls
to remake them.

Perhaps that was always you
a sculptor
crafting souls
in your own image.

Finally, in a spasm
you sliced a potter's knife
through the heart of your adopted family,
jagged gash through flesh.

There are no more heroes;
if Hercules were alive today
he'd be molesting young girls
between each of his labors.

But it was nothing like that
back when the world was fresh
with deep thoughts from a billion books.

That spring of hope
etched in black and white, in brilliant color,
in cinemascope with stereophonic sound,
back when Manhattan glittered with art and promise
when Woody met Annie.

Sweet Dream

In a dream I am held up at gunpoint.
The mugger is white.
Yes! In the depths of my unconscious
I am not a Racist!
The mugger is female.
Yes, I am empowering women!
The mugger is gay.
Yes, I am not engaging in harmful stereotypes of ineffectual
homosexuals!
The most Politically Correct dream Ever!

I Am Nobody And I Like It That Way

i am not a White Supremist
i am not a Nazi
i am not a Zionist
i am not a nationalist
i am not a patriot
i am not an American
i am not a good citizen of planet Earth
i am not a Jew
i am not a lapsed jew
i am not a Muslim
i am not a dabbler in Buddhism
i do not worship eternal Vishnu
i am not an atheist
i am not a fundamentalist
i am not an agnostic
i am not an occasional church goer
i am not a humanist
i am not a spiritualist
i am not a nihilist

i am part of the ecosphere
the web of life
doing my own small part
to destroy it

Why I will never get a DNA test

I know who I am!
My family roots are everyone.
I am Gandhi
I am Hitler
I am billions of
the obscure
each with our own
tale
each unknowable,
a contradiction inside a riddle inside an enigma.
I am she am they am we am he am us am who
am I?

Social Justice Worrier

Like Sisyphus, I awake every day
glance at that boulder
then crane my neck,
gaze up at
that high mountain peak.

Most days I decide
the boulder
is too big, too heavy,
the destination
too distant.

Once every millennium or so
I throw myself against it,
strain my body
from my fingertips to the tips of my toes,

push desperately
again, again, again, again, again,
the little engine that couldn't.

The boulder doesn't move
an infinitesimal fraction of a nanometer.

Even if, in a trillion millennia
this obstinate rock
too vast to be conceived
that casts no shadow
that throws shade everywhere

somehow made it to that distant peak
it would, I surmise
split and plummet
in a spinning arc
down, down, down, down, down.

On a planet of glittering distractions,
bread and circuses in every room,
in the palm of the hand,
why waste my day
with an immovable object
when I feel like
the most stoppable force
in the universe?

Me, Myself, and a Few Others

The Lake Isle of I'm Asleep

I will arise and go now
and go to I'm asleep,
and wondrous dreams I'll smell there
dredged up from islands deep.

Yes, wondrous lands I'll taste there
of pungent cinnamon
from east of wakefulness, where
all consciousness is gone.

My soul will float so far from here
in the ethereal mist
I just might find Nirvana,
I'll be totally blissed.

And marvelous beasts I'll hear there
and vegetation bright
from curving trees to buzzing bees
to glowing eyes at night.

I will arise and journey
far from this fractured place
to doves and love and glory
woven from inner space.

I may remain forever
and thrice as long again
in distant country of self
where there's no here or when.

Help, I am a human trapped within the body of a human!

Is this body my identity?
I didn't choose it. Did it choose me?
Without me it lacks agency.
Without it, I can never simply be.
Yet who's this "I," who is this "me"?
Am I my face? My personality?
Am I my thoughts that stream incessantly,
the sum of all that others think of me?
I feel that I must scream abundantly!
I wish my thoughts could fly and stream freely,
across far more than this vast galaxy,
outside this shell that aches so frequently.
Help please, I'm trapped in this body.
What is this "I"? Who, what, and woe is me!

Now is the Far Future

When I was small,
the smallest of all
—so small I can't remember how tiny I was,
perhaps not even a fetus, perhaps—
I figured out how old I'd be
in the year 2000.

Horrifying!
An ancient, wizened figure with an endless white beard
curved and boomeranging
thin and pointing in uncountable directions,
twisted spaghetti,
a garden of forking paths,
Jackson Pollack on my face
in multiple dimensions.

It's 2019 and I am a citizen of the far future
clutching not a magical staff but a small tablet
of infinite wisdom
and infinite foolishness
more omnipresent than a wizard's familiar.

I'm no ancient figure nasty with knowledge;
I know only how much I know I don't know.
I am endlessly young
a fetus perhaps
casting and scattering words
in intricate mazes of ignorance
disguised as knowledge.

"Feeling the Misery of Biting Fleas?"
— advertisement

I do feel their misery
the poor biting fleas
their lives are so short
and lacking in meaning.

I wonder if biting fleas undergo existential crises.
I doubt it.
They are not bright enough.

I will feel their existential crises
for them.

At least briefly
and in very small way.

Why I Have Wasted My Life

1,276 roads (or thereabouts) diverged
in a yellow wood
and I
just stood there, befuddled.

Thinking of Spring in the Fall

the seasons melt
heat wave, cold snap

somehow the trees know to
leave leaf litter, solemn sacrifice
for future plants, future planet

it's all tied to the circular motions
of our Earth
dancing on an invisible axis
tenacious on its annual trip
led by god's unerring hand,
the unwavering laws of physics

the seasons are subtly different
change creeps forward
the trees maintain their rhythms
more or less

brilliant reds and oranges
roughly on schedule

in spring adolescents break out
yearning for love
to leave their own gift to the
cursed future

the command "be fruitful and multiply"
is ages past
its expiration date

my spring long past
I ponder when to rake up
the annual sacrifice
prepare the lawn for
another next year

my spring is long past
my leaves long shed
barren and in fall now
I have left no gift to the future
no new mouths to suck
energy from our tired
mother earth

still I remember, yearn a little
each day as the planet spins

My Wife Eats Grapes While I Sit in the Dark

I have had my fill
of grapes, of poetry.

I could be struggling to spit out some verse,
paltry words
that express
nothing new.

My life is small,
contained.

I ate grapes earlier that
I had thought to leave for my wife.

They were delicious
so sweet
and so cold.

The coldness of death.

Death of a Calico

Callie died peacefully in a cardboard box on Christmas day. Her body convulsed gently, her face remained sweet, like she was asleep, and the orange and brown swirls and that delightful white belly conveyed her spirit. Small flecks of foam gathered at her lips. A stream of urine stained the box.

Callie, born in a manger (or at least a barn in Indiana).

Callie, died December 25 2019, 11 PM, Rockville, Maryland, USA.

Callie, born in a manger, but her mother was no virgin.

Perhaps she will live on, a set of bones clambering over furniture, bookshelves, the high frontier of the refrigerator, where her spirit gazes over the house.

More likely she will be obliterated, like a hundred billion cats before, less than a ripple in time's enormous tide.

We left the body on the back porch; overnight, it stiffened in the cold. The morning light revealed a scrawny, frigid corpse. I dug a hole just wide enough, just deep enough, dragged the box over, dumped in the corpse, a perfect fit.

Poor old thing.

Poor sweet thing.

No use for that body anymore.

No use for that body.

I cried as I shoveled the dirt back over, then tamped it down.

* * *

Thelma meows repeatedly every day for a month.

"Your sister cat is gone," I tell her. "Gone, gone. Gone forever. Gone."

* * *

Periodically, I feel overwhelmed, on the verge of weeping waterfalls. We all should be, all the time, at the weight of grief in the world. But we go on. There's much to do, and joy among the sorrow, new marriages and kittens. Waterfalls.

My Pandemic

My pandemic was a lovely pandemic. I had mountains of time to curl up with our sweet cat as her purring vibrated like a peaceful, gentle earthquake. I got to teach classes on Zoom, without rushing out of the house through sun and snow and showers in a rabid frenzy. Instead, I became a navigator of technology, skillfully switching between students, PowerPoints, whiteboards, videos, and breakout rooms. In virtual poetry and boardgame sessions, I traded thoughts and jokes with an array of old friends and new acquaintances from as far away as Canada, Italy, and even Nigeria. When it felt safe, I did get outside to play tennis with real people (while socially distanced), sprinting and cursing and laughing and leaping.

Throughout my pandemic, my wife and I took long strolls through the neighborhood, bantering about life's whimsical and tragic details. We revisited and re-revisited Maryvale Park, gazing over its wetlands, beginning in Spring with its cool and gentle warm breezes, new shoots of life, the first flashes of frogs and turtles and, in the nearby pond, fish squirming like giant sperm. We gazed at Summer wetlands bursting with flowers and reeds, from scrawny to verdant and wild, blossoming lushness that hid the progress of our favorite turtle below, while above an occasional blackbird flashed red wings. We lingered over Fall with its array of colors, flowers wilting and littering the ground, V formations of geese honking above on their journey toward the sun. We shivered through lonely icy empty Winter, stubs of brown reeds and trash fringing the exposed wetlands, cold still water with ice fragments below. And back to Spring, an occasional lonely hawk soaring the bright sky circling for prey, reminding us that nature is omnipotent and death always near.

My pandemic was a lovely pandemic. Too bad so many people suffered from loneliness, isolation, domestic violence, job loss, anxiety, depression, eviction. Too bad so many suffered from headaches, muscle aches, dizziness, struggle for breath, hospitalization, isolation, intubation. It's almost enough to ruin the whole pandemic!

With a Whimper

As I get older, parts start to rust,
the stomach rumbles,
the shoulders stiffen,
the ankles ache,
finally, the back that holds it all together
creaks toward oblivion.

My own tiny contribution
to the death of the universe.

Forgetting

After we die
people will say
from time to time
"Remember that couple?
They seemed to have had a good life
together."

Then a few years later
people won't say anything
at all.

Metaphysics of Poetry

Fruitflies Are Eternal, Poems Die Every Instant

So many poets, so few readers.

Poems are born and die at an exponentially accelerating rate.

The lucky ones flock to their internet homes
where they're downloaded by 3 people each,
glimpsed for 15 or 20 seconds,
flickering impulses of our collective conscious
lost to eternity.

Many are gorgeous
expressing the most profound impulses
of the human soul.

Free Verse

Is verse ever really free?
It costs time and psychic energy.

If you write too much,
won't your vital life juices be drained,
your energy emptied,
like a Coke can left on a road,
splashing a few feeble drops of quick energy
sizzling on hot asphalt?

What if we each have a limited stock of words,
a word bank that we'll one day expend?

Some say free verse is like playing tennis without a net.
Others say you construct the net and rules as you play.

I worry that I write in free verse because I am too lazy to follow
the rules of meter and rhyme. I worry that I write poetry be-
cause I am too lazy to create the narrative and character of
stories. I worry that I write stories because I am too lazy to do
the hard research of nonfiction prose. I worry that I write
nonfiction prose because I lack the imagination to write poetry.

If verse today is free, what will verse tomorrow be?

This is a Poem Because I Say It Is

This isn't a poem because it has rhyme or meter or line breaks or figurative language or breathtaking, heart-stopping epiphanies or anything associated with poetry. The muse isn't singing here, there are no profound imaginative leaps, no negative capability, no emotion recollected in tranquility, no words singing out despair, desire, ecstasy, no voyages to far-flung lands or to the frozen sea within. Nothing but dry words, brittle as twigs in a drought ready to burst into flame in the unlikely event that lightning strikes or if some careless camper unleashes a spark, leading to vast forest fires that all of humanity's exertion and ingenuity can't quench. Nothing poetic is here. Nevertheless, it's still a poem. It's like Humpty Dumpty said, but in a different way: "When I use a word, it means just what I choose it to mean — neither more nor less." When I write a poem, it is just as poetic as I want it to be, regardless of form or content. This is a poem because I say so!

Idea:

Rewrite Elizabeth Bishop's "The Fish" word for word,
but change the last line
from "And I let the fish go!"
to "And I had a delicious dinner!"

Poems from the Ancients

Shakespeare, Whitman, Yeats
gods proclaiming
eternal words

trumpets
in the ear
of the soul

Poets today
are callow children
straining like Sisyphus
to say something real,
profoundity, profanity
not pretty ditties, not witty, just pretty shitty

Struggling to string together
eternity by
uttering
fluttering, stuttering, sputtering words

Angels will not
recite their poems

500 years ago, adolescent Will Shakespeare
raging with hormones and his own self-importance
strained to make music
out of paltry
words words words

Poem in Limbo

My poem is not in heaven, my poem is not in hell.
Like scores of dozens of thousands of others,
like the stars strewn across the cold night sky
awaiting a dawn that may never come,
My poem is in limbo.

The somewhat important journal
where I sent my poem,
a desperate love letter
yearning for a great big YES,
will not answer its urgent plea.
There is no Yes,
There is no No,
There is only silence.

I dressed my poem in a saucy name
like a good-natured wench,
gave it an odor
like stinky cheese.

My poem is
shards of glass
glistening with promise
dazzling in the morning light
yearning to cut you.

My poem is
a plaintive flute in the pre-dawn,
a screaming trumpet scaring you awake.

My poem is silent.

My poem is
a love letter,
perhaps waylaid by bandits on a road at dusk.

My poem is
a long-ago love
I kissed only once,
never quite bedded.

I have forgotten my poem's features,
the color of its eyes, the texture of its lips
the shape and feel of its body
the perfume of its sweat.

My poem sits benumbed
with throngs of desperate souls
gazing at heaven.

Oh No, Not More Nature Poems!

Why

why e-
ven both-
er life sucks go-
ing on is point-
less might as well sleep for-
ev-
er
and
ever

Outside the window, bumblebees hover
above wild purple flowers

Lines Written at Seneca Creek State Park

Arching tree bent over double.
an old lady?
a cat stretching?
the entrance to a church.

* *

O little stream,
       why do you run so rapid?
You can't outrun the world.

* *

Gnarly roots form
steps along the path.
An old woman's
arthritic hands.

* *

Rounded rockface riven
                        with moss & lichen
primeval turtle,
megafauna return.

* *

Yellow and white wildflowers freckle the landscape.
Only two colors?
My restless soul
                          demands a rainbow.

* *

River runs over rocks,
swirls and eddies.
A Van Gogh painting?
God's washing machine?

* *

small sea
of ferns
why don't tiny dinosaurs dance
among you?

The Blue Jay and the Tuxedo Cat

A blue jay and a tuxedo cat outside the big picture window.

I thought, "My, what an excellent subject for a poem or a short story,
one that ends with the cat licking its lips, feathers fluttering
on wisps of empty air,
feathers
slowly floating,
floating slowly."

As it happened, the blue jay was perched on a high branch, oblivious.
The cat, warm and fuzzy, ambled along, half cartoon, half pet.

I knew that the cat was a wild creature,
wild in spirit, wild at heart,
painted in a tuxedo disguise,
hunting for its supper.

I yearned for the cat to survive,
on a diet of cartoon birds,
not the gorgeous jay
blue as blue,
preening itself on a high branch.

The cat would live,
for a while,
on small rodents
and unlucky birds
that came too close.

The blue jay and the tuxedo framed eternally
in the wide picture window,
opposite corners of a verdant painting.

Aesthetic Delights of the Coronavirus

That pale blue ball with buoyant red spikes
ubiquitous
familiar
has become
almost comforting
a beach ball
a child's toy
fantastic floating figure
intricate geometric model
artist's masterwork spiked by fervid imagination
vehicle of death in some sprawling sci-fi odyssey
floating free in outer space.

That familiar blue ball with buoyant red spikes
haunts our dreams
melts into our
unknowns.

To a Valley, *a mutant sonnet*

Our rolling planet is alive;
its effervescent skin shivers.
Multiple organisms thrive,
dancing strong in fields and rivers.

There's a crack in a canyon with cavernous cliffs
where the firm earth grips entangled roots.
Wildflowers blossom like spooky jazz riffs;
a spikey globe projects flowery shoots.

A bee descends as from a star,
hovers above awaiting flower,
sucks down life-giving nectar,
sustenance that will empower.

Colorful seas quiver with life;
amid them looms a lonely rock,
far from the distant city strife,
far from coronavirus shock.

Upon our slowly rolling Earth
the landscape hungers toward rebirth.

They have made worms' meat of me. — Mercutio

Dirt

A cornucopia of sensation
colorless
grainy and cool
fine, grainy chocolate
home
to worms

to the touch
dirt is all
delicate sensation
cool
moist
a map filled with
meaning
feeling incarnate
to those who are
one giant gland
blind and pulsating
sensing
through the soil
tending
loosening and enriching
the first farmers
the final farmers
true stewards of the
Earth

dirt
their home their world
rich organic
complex
a smooth cup
of coffee
laced with
roots
that they nourish
shoots
small, tender
the base of
life
a loving
grainy
substance

nurturing
common as itself
unique in the universe
base of the food chain
nucleus of the
web of life
farmed by
blind nurturing beings
who love us
who exist, subsist
at the
forgotten
center of the
universe
root of it all.

Two Plums

I ate two plums
        took them in
made them part of
myself
sucked their flowing juices
like the breasts on a

                            young mother

The first plum was sweet, succulent, life-giving
The second, bitter

      still my hunger is never satiated and I
consumed it bite by
                      bite

Did the bitter plum have less to offer?
Was it less nourishing?
Wasn't it gathered
             from the same tree?

Didn't it flow from the same
                  ever present
                            mother?

Plastic Bag

There's an ethereal beauty
in a plastic bag descending from the heavens,
an angel dancing in a strong wing
on its mystical journey
to choke
a nearby stream

Oh No, Not Another Nature Poem!

What more is there to say.
The hills are hilly
the grass is grassy
    and still inexplicable
as in Whitman's day.

Leaves lie like litter, individual as snowflakes
each a jagged, textual miracle,
    woven, a brown blanket
    future fertilizer
    for new leaves of grass.

Occasional birds twitter
    a snatch of song
    a suite
of call-and-response.

The grass is brown now,
the vegetation sparser, the songs quieter than decades past
when legions whipped up a chaotic orchestra
chirps, blades, thrums, green shoots.

In the distance, cars hum
    as they have, it seems, for time immemorial.

A tiny spider descends
from some invisible string
lands on my notebook
skitters across these words as I write,

disappears off the edge,
reappears crawling up my jacket.

I would flick it away, but it's so tiny
and fewer spiders crawl each day.
Once upon a time,
bugly hordes seethed, common as words scrolling a computer screen.
Now each minute life is precious.

In the distance, a lone hawk
prowls the sky.
How must if feel to fly?
        not in some contraption, but
borne aloft on one's own flesh?

Columns of trees loom every whichway
naked in the late fall
unashamed.

Hills roll into the horizon.

This was a golf course once.

Soon
it'll be townhouses.

Nature's encroachments
are
puny and sporadic.

So you see, I'm no Wordsworth or Whitman
not just through lack of talent.
These days,
poems celebrating nature's grandeur
are an affront.

This poem is a hymn in its feeble way
to glorious remnants
fading, fading, fading.

Endless Loop

A Very Short Collection of Very Short Poems

A Short Poem About Sleeping

zzz

An Extremely Short, Solipsistic, and Uninspiring Version of Song of Myself

I

Poem that Is Just a Title

Why I Write Prose Poems
I want to be a novelist but am too damn lazy.

The End

.

Yoga

My wife
contorts her body into eccentric shapes:
pretzels,
mobius tubes,
Klein bottles,
seven-dimensional dodecahedrons

My wife
becomes a spiritual being
levitates to distant
lands,
planets,
galaxies,
universes,
floats past spooky UFOs
sees intensely
the blinding light that cannot be seen
beauty
truth

I hate yoga
contorting my aging body
into ungainly shapes

straining to clear my mind
cluttered with a thousand layers
of pain
that job I never got
my sister-in-law who insulted me

I can never be in the moment
only lost among the litter of
a thousand moments past
cluttering my consciousness
choking my soul

Ghosts wail inside
my burdened brain

I will never be a spiritual being
at least until
the moment my withered body
ceases

Aphorisms

If you live long enough, you'll eventually make every stupid mistake possible. You'll learn from the mistakes, but in time you'll grow complacent and forget what you've learned.

Negative 273 degrees Fahrenheit is the coldest it is physically possible to be. On a negative 272 degree day, the optimist says "It could be worse"!

It is better to say something a little stupid some of the time than to remain silent.

An unfortunate side effect of getting a job that one has greatly desired is that you are now expected to work hard.

We need one eye on the future, one eye on the past, and one eye on the present. Unfortunately, most of us only have two eyes and so we wander through life in a state of confusion.

Every sentence I say is poetry. It's just that most of it is really, really bad poetry.

Planet Earth is dying and I don't feel so good myself.

Time

"Time ticks away faster than you think."
"Actually, time doesn't tick. It's clocks that tick. Time is silent."
"Or perhaps time is every noise in the world."

time is an egg
sunny-side up
slipping across
a slick griddle
running, running, running
away

time fries, time dies
time fritters
time flutters
time titters
time stutters

time is linear
time is chaos
time is everywhere and all things
time is nowhere, man
flowing through its nowhere land

time ain't on my side
time makes me run and hide
time out of mind
hurry up please, it's time

Do Not Read this Poem, Read the One Below

This poem is pathetic.
It has nothing to say and says it badly.

This poem has no rhythm, no rhyme, no resonance, no romance,
no reason.

However you spend your day,
do not read this poem!

Instead, read the poem below.
Its profound wisdom
will enlighten you.

The poem below will act as
your Zen Master
guiding you on a marvelous journey
on a craggy path through the mist
to the sun-drenched peak above,
where you will glimpse the universe.

Read the poem below and you are 110%, fully, completely, and
utterly guaranteed to

- find your bliss
- fulfill your destiny
- transcend time and space
- attain Nirvana

Don't Even Glance at This Poem, Read Only the One Above

You are a fool
to look at these words
written by a suffering man
with a migraine headache
a tortured childhood
and no sense of form or beauty.

I warn you
do not read this poem!
It is a profound waste of time,
precious seconds you will never recover
in the brief candle
that is
your life.

Instead, read the poem above
destined to stand
as the most profound work of artistic perfection
in the English
or any
language,

indeed, the most profound work,
visual, sculptural, musical, culinary, olfactory,
in the whole entire history
of artistic endeavor
in the known

and unknown
universe.

Eat, drink, observe, touch, taste, hear, the divine words of
the previous poem.
Feel the sublime experience
radiate
in every micrometer of your being
from the tips of your ears to the hangnails on your pinkie toes.
Satisfying
your body.
Satiating
your soul.

Lick the above poem,
rub your fingers lovingly
over each profound letter
feel the texture
enhanced by immortal words.

Print it out and bring it with you
into your daily shower.
Use it to gently scrub your body,
every cranny,
every pore,
every nanometer,
of your tender flesh,
each iota
of your immortal soul.

Coda

I Garden Weeds

I wouldn't say I have a brown thumb.
Fresh green weeds spring up where I garden,
infiltrating
the flowering natives.

I cultivate a wild look,
but when does the cultivation end
and weedy wildness begin?
What is art?
what is dishevelment?

All gardening means
tending living things
with tiny minds of their own,
selecting them, herding them,
eliminating undesirables,
bringing order to
wild, green beating hearts.

Writing poems
is a kind of gardening,
from the soil of the spirit.
What does one control?
Are weeds gifts from the wild?
from the oversoul?

To garden, one must get down in the dirt.
Never be afraid to prune,
as an old girlfriend, of sorts, told me.

She pulled out men as abruptly
as I yank dandelions the instant I spot
their lovely, golden heads.

In the main garden bed,
I scrape out, dig out, wrench out
weeds, weeds, weeds, weeds.
Gnarly little interlopers
with fluffy white flowering balls,
viny running weeds, encircling,
boisterous, broad-leafed things,
puny patches of innocent clovers.

As one wise gardener said,
a weed is just a plant that has not found a champion.

No matter how I prune and pull
the soil of my soul
I've lost control
of my garden,
my unruly thoughts,
dreams, wild words.

Ungrateful little weeds
peek out,
smile,
say, "don't hurt us,
we are
gifts of nature
who made us all."

Native Americans Return to the Suburbs

Native Americans tread, creep, sprint, and leap
through America's suburbs.

Rabbit nibbles incessantly on vast salad bowls,
breeds copiously on a million lawns,
watches nervously for enemies, Cat and Car,
feels a rush of adrenaline, strange joy as
she dashes into a thicket.

Rabbit suckles her babies,
loves them deeply, forgets them quickly,
remembers the centuries, lives in the now.

Deer no longer dwells in shadows,
hiding from her
ancient friend, ancient nemesis:
humans,
for whom she has, time and again and again,
kindly provided nourishment.

Nowadays, Deer eyes two-legged beasts,
common as the stars,
as curiosities
if not quite
friends.

Clever Fox hunts from the hidden places,
preserves the gardens of her tidy human neighbors
from Rabbit's ravages.

Fox remembers her long-lost cousin, Wolf,
slaughtered and confined to
reservations.

Fox mourns Wolf, but cannot
Howl!

Crow struts boldly down gray streets,
steps nimbly between killer machines,
dines greedily on road kill,
digests corpses of Squirrel, Chipmunk, Rabbit, Deer.

Flying into nearby yards, meadows, Crow
returns her cousins to the soil from which they sprang.

Crow remembers Raven, clever thief
who stole the sun,
to alleviate humanity's
suffering.

Native Americans live among us,
if one knows where to look,
ghosts, spirits, remnants
of 50 million dead,
Mohawk, Cherokee, Sioux, Ojibwe, Pawnee, Diné,
countless more, names forgotten.